101

Q & A

For Sigmund Freud

By

John Griffin

Time Spent With Cats Is Never Wasted,

Sigmund Freud

Dedicated To:

My wife, Kathleen, whose belief in me carried me through this effort,

My daughters, Jennifer and Kaitlyn, who are my world,

My grandchildren, Mackenzie and Savannah, who put smiles on my face,

My brother, Jim, who has been an inspiration,

Prudence Allen, M.D., who listened to my ramblings, offering me comfort and a place to vent,

Laurie Zelas, my newest "ear",

My Buddy, Colm, who has endured me in our many coffee chats,

My two cats whose affection warmed me, especially Cedric, my lap cat.

Preface:

This short tome was inspired, by all things, rejection. I am quite sure that Freud would have something to say about my motivation. Did my motivation emanate from a subtle unconscious need to combat this rejection? What was this rejection? I made application to a local State university to pursue a Master's degree in psychology. I was, as you can guess, rejected on my initial attempt. Not being content with that, I requested an appeal and was turned down once again.

My interest in the field of psychology goes way back to my high school days. The psyche of the human person is wonderfully exciting to me. The human personality is fascinating to me. So, I did a little research to find out where to start my own independent studies and one name in the field of psychology/psychiatry kept coming up: Sigmund Freud. Every corner of my research or book that I picked up had some mention of Freud. It was a delightful discovery. These discoveries spurred me on to explore Freud and explore I have done. My studies of Freud have been very fruitful and insightful. He has become, in a way, my mentor. This is not to say that I agree with everything he wrote or said but I do pay homage to much of his works. Freud is now an integral component in my thinking and being.

In writing this Q & A book, I simply wanted to bring a brief familiarity to the reader and, perhaps, ignite a greater interest in Freud. I hope that this Q & A format will help to cement some details which will then act as an impetus to expand into wider studies. Also, please note that these questions are in no chronological order. I am not a psychologist or medical doctor. I am a layman with a passion for Freud. This is not a strict biography per se. Also, the reader will find one page per question. This was a deliberate construct of mine so that you, the reader, can jot down any ideas or thoughts to help you in your Freudian studies. Cheers to your wonderful journey!

1. When was I born?

I was born May 6, 1856. My full given name was Sigismund Schlomo Freud. Also, I am very fond of Darwin who had many journeys this year of 1836, and who finally returned to England after being away for five years. Darwin would factor heavily one day in shaping my personal philosophy.

2. Who were my parents?

My father, who was Jewish, was named Jakob. My Mother, Amalia (formerly Nathanson), gave birth to my seven siblings. I had six sisters and one brother.

3. Did I have a nickname at birth?

Yes, I was born with a crop of thick black hair. Seeing this, my mother called me her "little moor". My mother doted on me and believed that, one day, I would be famous and accomplish great things. At age twenty two I formally changed my first name to Sigmund.

4. How much did my mother dote on me?

Well, one day my sister was playing the piano and I could not stand the noise. I was not fond of music as it is but to have it in our apartment was too much. I asked my mother to stop it and, sure enough, there was no more piano noise ever again as mother put an end to it.

5. Where was I born?

In the town of Freiberg in the country of Moravia which is now called Pribor of the Czeck Republic. Moravia was part of the Great Austrian-Hungarian Empire.

6. Was my surname always "Freud"?

No, it was not. History shows t it may have been "Freund" some generations ago and the "n" was dropped.

7. How many wives did my father, Jakob, have in his lifetime?

Jakob had three wives. By his first marriage, he had two sons, Emanuel and Phillip. There were no children in the second marriage and as stated above, there were eight children in his third marriage.

8. Did my family and I always live in Moravia?

No, at age 4, my father moved us to Vienna (Austria) where I stayed for quite some time. Eventually, after getting my degree in medicine, I moved to Berggasse 19, 1090 Wien Vienna IX in 1891 where I stayed for forty seven years.

9. Was I gifted as a child?

Yes, I excelled at all my academics. Many people probably do not know that I actually have a photographic memory. I graduated Summa Cum Laude from High School.

10. Is it true that my father's behavior and persona catapulted me into seeking success?

Yes. There is a very common tale told about my father and me. He and I were walking down the street one day and a stranger knocked my Dad's off into the mud and made a disparaging remark about us Jews. My father did not fight back and only picked up his hat and went his merry way. I saw this as weakness and vowed not to be pushed around like that.

11. Did I have any heroes?

Yes. The Great Hannibal. I could relate to Hannibal as a Semite. As well, Hannibal defeated the Romans prior to Rome's Catholic birth as Freud had a distaste for Rome and a hatred for Catholicism.

12. Despite my hatred for Roman Catholicism, didn't my Nanny take me to morning Catholic Mass?

Yes. I had a Nanny, an older rather unattractive woman who would take me to daily Catholic Mass. Thus, I did have exposure to the smells and bells of Catholicism and to its Saints. Rumor has it that Nanny was let go for stealing and arrested.

13. Was psychiatry my first choice of profession?

No, it wasn't. It was in my head to study law but I changed my mind. I did do a bit of dabbling in different fields like zoology, physiology and philosophy.

14. What did my mother and father do for a living?

My father was a wool merchant and not too successful a one. My mother was, as was the custom in those days, a homemaker.

15. Did I ever marry?

Yes, I did. We had a long engagement of about five years as I was not financially set to enter into a marriage. My wife's name was Martha Bernay's. She gave birth to our six children.

16. What were my children's names?

They were Oliver, Ernst, Sophie, Clemens, Anton and Anna.
Anna was the only one who did not marry nor had children.

17. Which one of my children would follow in his father's footsteps?

Anna was the only one of my children to follow me into the world of psychoanalysis. It is intimated that my beloved Anna may have had lesbian tendencies. I was more open to this type of behavior than my colleagues. She is however the only direct relative that I ever psychoanalyzed.

18. In what field did I initially train?

I trained as a neurologist. But, during this time, stirrings arose in me with an interest in the human mind.

19. What other field did I have a strong passion for?

I loved the field of archaeology and acquired a great many artifacts of antiquity. Some might even say that I read more on archaeology than psychology.

20. What do I believe that all people seek?

I am firmly convinced that all people seek inner peace in their unique ways.

21. How many cigars did I smoke daily?

It would not be uncommon to find me having smoked over twenty cigars in one day in my youth.

22. So, was there any drawback to my constant smoking?

Yes, I came down with severe cancer of my right jaw.

23. What did I think smoking was a substitute for another activity?

I believed that smoking was a substitute for masturbation. I, however, did not apply this belief to myself. I personally held to a personal position of sexual abstinence. I do admit this is a bit hypocritical.

24. What cigars did I generally smoke?

A trabuco, which is small and mild, was my common choice due to Austrian import restrictions. Otherwise, I would, as often as I can, inhale a nice Don Pedro or Cubana.

25. When did I finally emigrate to England and where?

On June 6, 1938, I arrived in London, England, at Victoria Station.

26. For what reason did I make my one and only visit to the United States?

I was invited to lecture at Clark University in Worcester, MA in 1909 and was granted an Honorary doctorate by the institution.

27. What was my feelings about America?

I was not fond of their Capitalism system which seemed to bring everything down to a competition and to dollars and cents. I said that America had "dollaria".

28. Did I like anything about America?

I was a big fan of Mark Twain and read his works. Also, America did play a role in my emigration to England so I can be grateful for that.

29. Why did I continue smoking even though I knew it aggravated my cancer?

I kept smoking because I believed it helped me to think better - "food for thought" - I called it.

30. Did I suffer badly from my jaw cancer?

Yes, it got so bad that eventually I had permanent hearing loss in my right ear. I had to put my therapist's chair at the end of my patient's couch just to hold effective sessions.

31. Where did I reside at the time of my death?

I lived at 20 Maresfield Gardens. As well, this residence now houses the London Freud Museum.

32. What was one of my favorite leisure activities?

It was a card game called "Tarock". Yes, these are the infamous tarot cards but they were long played as a card game before taking on an air of divination.

33. How did I acquire my now famous therapist couch?

Actually, it was a gift from my patient, a Mrs. Benvenisti, in 1891 and it has stayed with me.

34. What did the Royal Charter Society do for me that was practically unheard of?

Representatives of the Royal Charter Society brought the book physically to me to sign. This type of recognition was reserved for royalty, like kings. To come to me was a deep sign of reverence really.

35. What special document did I need to emigrate to England in 1938?

A *Unbedenklichkeitserklarung* is a statement made about the emigrating party that states there is no impediment. I did have my passport back by this time already though.

36. What psychopathic leader feared me?

Hitler did not have me arrested. To leave I actually was coerced into signing a statement that the Gestapo treated me fairly. Seeing as I was not arrested and the other parties emigrating were also freed, it was a small price to pay and not completely disingenuous.

37. Did I love dogs?

Yes. I actually did not have my first dog until I was into my seventies. I was fond of the Chow breed of dog. The dog that I had up until my passing was named Lun. Lun would sit in with me during sessions.

38. What interesting observation did I make about having one of my dogs present during sessions?

I could visibly see that clients were less tense and anxious with the dog around.

39. Is it true that I had a bit of misanthropic nature?

Yes, I did hold man in contempt and I, for the most, kept a close circle of friends. I generally, though, required loyalty to me from my colleagues. You may say that I had a steely confidence in my work and wanted to just pursue my teachings without hindrance.

40. Is it true that I had an affair with my wife's sister, who helped our household?

I choose not to say. There are rampant rumors that I did have a dalliance with my wife's sister. I will not deny that I found her attractive. Investigators turned up a hotel receipt where we were registered. But, as I say, no conclusive evidence. I practiced sexual abstinence.

41. What was one feature of my final residence at 20 Maresfield?

The property had eight bedrooms which was rather large for its age and it had electric lighting, which was a special amenity.

42. What are some of the most important teachings I left after my death?

I would not be bragging if I said that my complete works speaks innumerable volumes. One of my more famous works was <u>On Interpretations of Dreams</u> which set psychoanalysis into motion.

43. Did I ever suffer from neurosis?

Yes, many people are unaware that I suffered from my own neurosis for about a decade. As I viewed that neurosis was often caused by sexual abuse by the father in the childhood years, then I might have to be admitting that my father abused me sexually and I repressed these memories. This was a hard pill to swallow. I can be certain my father did not sexually abuse me.

44. Did I ever psychoanalyze myself.

Yes, I did and I came to know myself very well. I figured that I practiced what I preached by doing so.

45. Did I also experience an incident which struck me at the core of my being during childhood?

Yes, outside of my father's hat knocked off, I once came into my parents' bedroom at an early age and peed on their bed. My father got angry and told my mother, in front of me, that I would never amount to anything. From that day, I vowed to be a success.

46. What did I have to say about psychosexual development?

I divided human sexual development as the oral, anal, phallic, latent and genital stages.

47. What did I mean by "oral" stage?

A baby from birth to about one year of age is comforted suckling at his or her's mother's breast.

48. What did you mean by "anal" stage?

This I considered the age from about one year of age up to about three that a child gains control over bodily functions.

49. What did I mean by "phallic stage"?

From ages three to six, children now recognize their genitals and discover differences in the sexes. It is in this stage that my Oedipus complex is experienced.

50. What did I mean by "latent" stage?

Here, in age six to puberty sexual repression occurs and attention is paid to other life experiences and pleasures.

51. What did I mean by "genital" stage?

This starts in puberty and does not end until death. Normal heterosexual behavior occurs in this stage.

52. Weren't you also famous for the "Id", "Ego", and "Super-Ego (Over-I)"?

Yes, I was. Everyone I know attributes these to me.

53. So, is the "Id" a good thing?

I see it as such. It is our innate instincts at birth. It is our unconscious. It lurks in the shadows so to speak. It is the realm of my pleasure principle. It carries all the excitations of life.

54. What is my Pleasure Principle concept?

Actually, it is more properly referred to as the "pleasure-pain" principle. Here, the human person basically seeks to avoid pain or events which bring no pleasure. Development of the person leads to a growth in ego which puts the "pleasure-pain" principle into check with my "reality" principle.

55. What is this "Ego" that you write about?

If we think of the "Id" as the uncontrolled passions, we can then think of the "Ego" as common sense and reason. Ego is the practical part of our psyche.

56. What did you mean by "super-ego"?

I can explain it as self-criticism. It is, you could call it, the parent in us. It is the judgemental and rigid part of our psyche. An over-active super-ego can not necessarily be a good thing as it can hinder taking any action at all and, frankly, make life miserable.

57. What is this hysteria I write about?

I need to say that my hysteria is basically repressed memories in the unconscious pouring out exhibiting with strange behavior, sometimes violent outbursts or motor and sensory disturbances. . I advanced the idea that hysteria was due to past sexual mistreatment. I was later proved wrong. In fact I took criticism from my colleagues when I disagreed that hysteria was relegated to women only. The very word itself derives from Latin meaning "womb".

58. Did I use cocaine?

Yes, I did for a period of time from around 1884 to 1887. I actually was hoping to become famous and do a study of its beneficial qualities. Sadly, someone preempted me and stole the show. Actually, it turns out that cocaine is highly addictive and a colleague of mine got hooked. It is a chapter in my life which I would not take away as it was a time that I felt that I was using science in directly trying to help others.

60. What do people call me which I accept flatteringly?

I am referred to as the founder or father of psychoanalysis or psychiatry.

61. When did I "discover" psychoanalysis?

I saw the effects on a patient we gave (Dr. Joseph Breuer) this treatment to and it worked. We kept her anonymous as patient Anne O. but her name was really Bertha Pappenheim. This was around the period of 1880-1882.

62. What is psychoanalysis at its core?

It is known as the talking therapy. The patient eventually experiences a cathartic moment or more and it leads to better mental health.

63. What did I think about war?

I took a dour view of mankind. People have libidos. They are full of pent up aggressions. These aggressions can exhibit themselves as constructive or destructive. They can be inhibited by the Superego, resulting in guilt. They can spill outward into violence, such as rape, murder and war.

64. What ENT physician did I have a friendship with and frequent written correspondence?

That would be William Fleiss, M.D.. Our friendship lasted six years, from 1887 to 1903. Dr. Fliess performed operations on my nasal area to try to cure my neurosis. They did not work.

65. Was my correspondence with Dr. Fliess destroyed as I requested?

No. It was not. Princess Marie Bonaparte (yes, she is a relative of Napoleon Bonaparte) saw to it that they were preserved.

66. What did I name the original and premiere psychoanalytic society?

It was named the Wednesday Psychology Society in 1902. It met in my apartment on Wednesdays.

67. Did I change the name?

Yes, in 1908, it was changed to the Vienna Psychoanalytic Society.

68. Who were some more prominent members?

There were Alfred Adler, Carl Jung, Otto Rank, and others. Adler would be the first prominent figure to break away from me. Otto Rank was my right hand man for over twenty years and was second only to me in prolific writing.

69. What is this Oedipus Complex that I have made famous (or infamous)?

I simply assert that during the phallic stage a child begins to hate his father and sexually desire his mother, much like the Oedipus character known in fiction. For girls, during this stage, they experience penis envy.

70. What is this repression that I write about?

Repression basically means that you store away unwanted thoughts, ideas, conflicts etc. Into the unconscious mind. I have expressed my theory of repression as the cornerstone of all of psychoanalysis. It is one of many defense mechanisms.

71. What makes repression so important?

I make analogy of the human mind to that of an iceberg. As with an iceberg, only the tip of the mind shows above the water. I consider this the "conscious" mind with the remaining part underwater. This represents all other emotions, skills, ideas and the like that one does not really have an awareness of.

72. What was the case of Dora about?

I had a female patient given the anonymous name of "Dora" who I treated for hysteria but, ultimately, failed. I suspected that Dora was being sexually abused by a family friend.

73. What year did I first toss out the concept of "psychoanalysis"?

I chose that in 1896. Consequently, I also started analyzing my own dreams from about 1986 to 1899. It was time well spent.

74. What was the Reality Principle I espoused?

Basically, I believe the human person eventually moves from the Pleasure Principle of the Id to that of the Ego, and the outer world shapes behavior.

75: What did Josef Breuer think about my work as he was one of my mentors?

He and I collaborated but he did think that I overemphasized sexuality in much of my writings.

76. Of all people close to me that I would welcome writing my definitive biography, who would it be?

Ernest Jones is and has always been one of my closest friends and colleagues and my official biographer. Jones was a British neurologist and psychoanalyst. He was the first English speaking practitioner of psychoanalysis

77. What affectionate nickname did I give my children?

I called them my "little troop".

78. Which of my writings led most to the birth of psychoanalysis?

I wrote <u>On Interpretation of Dreams</u> in 1900 and thus it was born.

79. What was one of my favorite food dishes?

It was a dish called tafelspitz, which was boiled beef.

80. What vegetable did I like least?

I am not fond of cauliflower. In fact, I detested it.

81. What poultry did I not like?

I hated chicken.

82. What was my favorite dessert?

I enjoyed homemade vanilla ice cream.

83. Who did I put in charge of my household finances?

I put my wife in charge of running the household and finances. I still retained head of household status nonetheless. As well, our household had the assistance of my wife's, Martha's sister, Minna.

84. How was I able to write so prolifically?

I would usually stay up until about two in the morning. I also had the ability to fall asleep instantly, not a strong suit that many others had. I would wake up at the same time each morning and start my day.

85. What phobia did I suffer from?

I had a fear of railway travel. In fact, I would not ride in the same car as my family. I didn't publicize my phobia.

86. Is it true that I turned down a Hollywood Script?

Samuel Goldwyn of Hollywood offered me $100,000 to contract for a movie about love. I declined.

87. When did I publish "Beyond the Pleasure Principle"?

I published it in 1920. It was a landmark publication as it introduced my theory of the death wish, the "Thanatos".

.

88. What did this Thanatos represent?

Thanatos encompassed all the modes of destruction, repetition, aggression, compulsion and self-destruction.

89. So what is this "Eros" that I write about?

Eros is the drive of life, love, creativity, sexuality, self-satisfaction and species preservation.

90. Was I known to have a sense of humor?

Yes, actually, I had a good sense of humor. I wrote about my position on humor in a paper entitled <u>Jokes and Their Relation to the Unconscious</u>.

91. What did you mean by tendentious jokes and non-tendentious jokes?

Tendentious jokes are jokes which contain hostile or lustful themes or both. Non-tendentious jokes are jokes which have dual meanings, like saying "my heart bleeds for you" where heart not only means the physical bleeding but also the emotional pull of the heart string.

92. What famous practice did you bring to the treatment of mental health treatment?

I was the first to introduce a couch for my patients and, it may sound like nothing much, but I greeted my patients in a nice three piece suit. I said goodbye to the days of lab coats and barbaric treatment of mental patients.

93 What do you mean by barbaric treatment of mental patients?

In earlier days of practice, it was common practice to castrate male schizophrenic sufferers and to circumcise the clitoris from female hysterics.

94. How bad did my jaw cancer get in my final days?

It got so bad that those around me could smell the foul air of rotting flesh.

95. What are these defense mechanism I write about?

It is the mind's way of trying to mitigate or eliminate additional trauma.

96. What are my ten defense mechanisms?

They are: denial, displacement, intellectualization, projection, rationalization, reaction formation, regression, repression, sublimation and suppression.

97. Which are most popular?

Denial is frequent as we often see people simply not acknowledging the existence of a situation or problem. Rationalization occurs when we try to provide a logical explanation when the reality would reflect back unkindly on ourselves.

98. What quotes are attributed to me that I may never have said?

There is a quote which goes "Time spent with cats is never wasted. This is hard to believe since I did not like cats, preferring dogs. Also, I am quoted as having said "Sometimes a cigar is just a cigar" but no official record of that exists either.

99. What is my famous Freudian slip about?

I formally call them Fehlleistungen in German or parapraxis in Greek. These are things that we catch ourselves saying erroneously in mangling words or actions. The entering of unconscious ideas into the conscious mind is what I believe causes these Freudian slips.

100. Who was one of my disciples with whom I was very close but we broke our relationship off?

Carl Jung and I had a very, very close relationship but Carl had issues with having male relationships and the issue of displaced homosexual vibes. Jung was concerned whether he had homosexual love or erotic love for me and would inform me of these feelings. Jung also thought that Freud went too far in sexual matters in his theories. I really never stopped caring for Jung even after we split.

101. Was I buried?

I died on September 23, 1839. No, I was not buried. I was cremated. The urn chosen to house my ashes was from my own personal collection. It was a Greek urn from around 600 B.C. and it was kept in the Golders Green Mausoleum, London, England. Thieves attempted to steal this urn on January 15, 2014. Damage was done. Also, it is commonly thought that I used physician assisted suicide by asking my trusted physician Max Schur. M.D. to administer a lethal dosage of twenty one milligrams of morphine. Death came within hours.

Acknowledgements:

- BookCaps Study Guides, Sigmund Freud In Plain and Simple Language
- Reading Freud, Jean-Michel Quinodoz
- Freud: Great Thinkers on Modern Life, Brett Kahr
- The Death of Sigmund Freud, Mark Edmundson
- Freud: In his time and ours, Elizabeth Roudinesco
- Beyond the Pleasure Principle, Sigmund Freud
- Freud, Jonathan Lear
- Freud the Man, Lydia Flem
- Freud Dictionary of Psychoanalysis, Nandor Fodor & Frank Gaynor
- Wikipedia